A Note to Parents

DK READERS is a compelling prog[...] readers, designed in conjunction wi[...] experts, including Dr. Linda Gambr[...] Professor of Education at Clemson University. Dr. Gambrell has served as President of the National Reading Conference, the College Reading Association, and the International Reading Association.

Beautiful illustrations and superb full-color photographs combine with engaging, easy-to-read stories to offer a fresh approach to each subject in the series. Each DK READER is guaranteed to capture a child's interest while developing his or her reading skills, general knowledge, and love of reading.

The five levels of DK READERS are aimed at different reading abilities, enabling you to choose the books that are exactly right for your child:

Pre-level 1: Learning to read
Level 1: Beginning to read
Level 2: Beginning to read alone
Level 3: Reading alone
Level 4: Proficient readers

The "normal" age at which a child begins to read can be anywhere from three to eight years old. Adult participation through the lower levels is very helpful for providing encouragement, discussing storylines, and sounding out unfamiliar words.

No matter which level you select, you can be sure that you are helping your child learn to read, then read to learn!

LONDON, NEW YORK, MUNICH,
MELBOURNE, AND DELHI

DK UK

Series Editor Deborah Lock
Senior Art Editor Tory Gordon-Harris
U.S. Editor Elizabeth Hester
Design Assistant Sadie Thomas
Production Claire Pearson
DTP Designer Almudena Díaz
Jacket Designer Peter Radcliffe

Reading Consultant
Linda Gambrell, Ph.D.

First American Edition, 2003
This edition, 2014
Published in the United States by DK Publishing
345 Hudson Street, New York, New York 10014

14 10 9 8 7 6 5 4 3
004—197250—January/2014

A catalog record for this book is available
from the Library of Congress.

ISBN 978-1-4654-1674-2 (Paperback)
ISBN 978-1-4654-1675-9 (Hardcover)

DK books are available at special discounts when
purchased in bulk for sales promotions, premiums,
fund-raising, or educational use.
For details, contact:
DK Publishing Special Markets
345 Hudson Street, New York, New York 10014
SpecialSales@dk.com

Printed and bound in China
by South China Printing Company

The publisher would like to thank the following for their
kind permission to reproduce their photographs:
(Key: a=above; c=centre; b=below; l=left; r=right t=top)

2 Tracy Morgan: (crb). Ross Simms and the
Winchcombe Folk & Police Museum: (cra). Barrie
Watts: (br). 4 Corbis: Jeremy Horner (c). 6–7 Getty
Images: Mike Timo. 7 Barrie Watts: (br). 8 Tracy
Morgan: (bl). Corbis: Bill Ross (cl). 8–9 Getty Images:
Darrell Gulin. 9 Natural History Museum: (bcr).
10–11 Getty Images: Jerry Driendl.
11 Stephen Oliver: (bc). 12 Stephen Oliver: (bc), (br).
13 Judith Miller & Dorling Kindersley & Bonhams,
Edinburgh: (bl). 15 Getty Images: Tom King (tr).
Stephen Oliver: (bc). 16–17 Gables Travels. 17 Guy
Ryecart: (bc). 18–19 Stephen Oliver. 19 Stephen Oliver:
(br). Natural History Museum: (bcl). 21 Corbis: Craig
Tuttle (br). 22 Ross Simms and the Winchcombe Folk &
Police Museum: (br). 22–23 Jerry Young. 24–25 Jerry
Young. 25 Natural History Museum: (br). Jerry Young:
(c). 26 Stephen Oliver: (bl). 26–27 Getty Images: Terry
Husebye. 27 Getty Images: Paul Goff: (bl). 28 British
Museum: (br). 32 British Museum: (br).
Stephen Oliver: (c). Jerry Young: (bl)

All other images © Dorling Kindersley
For further information see: www.dkimages.com

Discover more at
www.dk.com

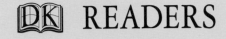
DK READERS

LEARNING TO READ

pre-level 1

Colorful
Days

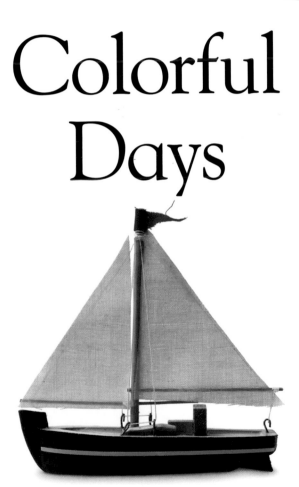

How many colors

green

yellow

pink

red

Come and
play with me.

can you see?

eye

nose

mouth

white

We can play
in the cold,
white snow.

We can look at the purple flowers.

leaf

purple

petal

9

blossom

We can run
around the trees
with the pink
blossoms.

pink

petal

eye

gray

12

ear

fur

We can pet
the small,
gray rabbits.

We can sail
with the boats
on the blue water.

mast

sail

blue

deck

We can walk
through the
tall, yellow
sunflowers.

 yellow

seeds

petal

orange

We can eat
a cold, orange
ice pop.

ice pop

stick

boots

red

We can kick
the leaves and
pick the red apples.

tree

jaw

leg

black

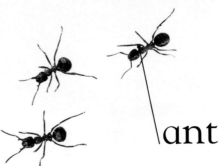
ant

We can crawl
like the ants and
the black beetle.

slimy skin

feet

brown

We can croak
like the small,
brown frogs.

branches

needles

green

We can run around
the tall, green trees.

We can hang
silver balls and
put on gold crowns.

 silver

glitter ball

jewel

gold

How many colors

can you see?

Picture Word List

white
page 6

purple
page 8

pink
page 10

gray
page 12

blue
page 14

yellow
page 16

orange
page 18

red
page 20

black
page 22

brown
page 24

green
page 26

silver and **gold**
page 28